THE RIGHT CAREER FOR ME

CARPENTER

KATHLEEN A. KLATTE

ROSEN PUBLISHING

Published in 2024 by The Rosen Publishing Group, Inc.
2544 Clinton Street, Buffalo, NY 14224

Portions of this work were originally authored by Greg Roza and published as *A Career as a Carpenter*. All new material in this edition was authored by Kathleen A. Klatte.

Cover Designer: Michael Flynn
Intertior Designer: Rachel Rising
Editor: Kathleen Klatte

Cataloging-in-Publication Data
Names: Klatte, Kathleen A.
Title: Carpenter / Kathleen A. Klatte.
Description: New York : Rosen Publishing, 2024. | Series: The right career for me | Includes glossary and index.
Identifiers: ISBN 9781499475753 (pbk.) | ISBN 9781499475760 (library bound) | ISBN 9781499475777 (ebook)
Subjects: LCSH: Carpentry--Vocational guidance--Juvenile literature. | Carpenters--Juvenile literature.
Classification: LCC TH5608.7 K53 2024 | DDC 694.023--dc23

Manufactured in the United States of America

CPSIA Compliance Information: Batch #CWRYA24. For further information, contact Rosen Publishing at 1-800-237-9932.

CONTENTS

INTRODUCTION

People first began using the modern word *carpenter* in the 14th century. Traditionally, carpentry has been defined as the art of building structures from wood. It's one of the oldest professions practiced in the world. Archaeologists in Germany have discovered wells with wooden casings that were built 7,000 years ago during the Neolithic Age. The wood shows signs of tool marks, where humans cut tree trunks into boards, then fitted the boards together with carefully carved joints.

So why is such an old career a good choice today? The answer is that buildings, no matter how sophisticated they've become, still require carpentry at various points in the construction process. Carpenters build the forms used to shape concrete foundations and timber frames for houses. They build walls, floors, and roofs, as well as things such as countertops and cabinets. Even in concrete and steel high-rise buildings, carpenters build interior walls and frame doorways. They also build scaffolding necessary for the construction process.

Some carpenters work on construction sites. Others specialize in handcrafted wooden furniture.

Some professions may experience a loss of work during difficult economic times when customers simply don't have the money to buy these goods and services. Even in a poor economy when people might not be able to afford new homes, carpenters are busy repairing and remodeling houses, offices, and other buildings. Today, buildings are constantly being renovated to accommodate new technology or to conform to energy-efficient standards. A trained carpenter can flourish in good economic times as well as bad. In addition, a carpenter can save money by doing his or her own home repairs, rather than hiring someone else. Read on to learn more about carpentry and carpentry professions.

NORM ABRAM, TV CARPENTER

Norm Abram is a master carpenter. He's been familiar to Public Broadcasting Service (PBS) television audiences since 1979. He was one of the original cast members of *This Old House*.

This Old House focuses on home renovations, usually for vintage houses. At 44 seasons, it predates, and has survived alongside the current craze of reality TV shows. It's one of the most respected home improvement shows in TV history and has received 19 Emmy Awards and 92 nominations. Abram was the show's master carpenter through 43 seasons.

In addition to his appearances on *This Old House*, Abram hosted 21 seasons of *The New Yankee Workshop*, also for PBS. The show focused on traditional woodworking and furniture building.

Abram wrote eight companion books for *This Old House*. He's also appeared on a variety of news and talk shows throughout the years. For his retirement from *This Old House* at age 73, he was honored with a PBS TV special titled *The House That Norm Built*.

He currently resides in Massachusetts with his wife in a Colonial house he built himself. He's also a member of the board of trustees for Old Sturbridge Village, a restored historic village in Sturbridge, Massachusetts.

Norm Abram was the master carpenter on the PBS TV show *This Old House* for 43 seasons, since its premier in 1979.

CHAPTER ONE

NOT JUST A HAMMER AND NAILS

Humans began using primitive tools to cut and manipulate wood millions of years ago. The earliest evidence of actual carpentry—building a structure from separate pieces of wood—dates back 7,000 years. Archaeologists have found evidence of timber longhouses in Europe from the Neolithic Age, 6,000 years ago. The oldest-surviving wooden building in the world was built in 607 CE.

Horyuji Temple in Nara, Japan, dates to 607 CE. It's considered the world's oldest wooden building and is a UNESCO World Heritage Site.

As humans invented new tools and new ways to manipulate the natural resources around them, they began to construct more complex things. Ancient Romans and Egyptians used timber for roofs. Early carpenters developed timber framing for buildings in the ninth century. Carpenters were some of the most skilled and respected craftsmen in the Middle Ages.

Stave churches are remarkable feats of carpentry. They're made entirely of wood—even the nails. Carpenters also built them using axes instead of saws. Historians estimate that Europeans built 1,000 to 2,000 of these churches between the 12th and 14th centuries. Today, 29 remain.

A restoration project used machine-made shingles, which failed. The thousands of shingles covering a stave church are all hewn by ax.

Today, carpenters still practice some medieval techniques. After all, anything that's stood for centuries is well worth studying! Some even specialize in recreating historic buildings for living history museums—or repairing historic structures such as Notre Dame cathedral which was badly damaged in a fire in 2019.

But what makes carpentry a good modern career choice? Quite a bit, actually. Carpenters construct the frames used for concrete foundations. They build the frame or skeleton of the house. They lay floors, build walls, frame windows and doorways, and build roofs. Modern carpenters work with materials besides wood—things such as plastic, fiberglass, and drywall. In fact, the carpenters union now includes other construction trades. A member of the carpenters union might well work with steel or concrete. They need to adapt to new trends such as solar power and smart technology.

Carpenters work on high-tech skyscrapers, too. They build scaffolding during construction and finish the inside of the building to make it suitable for use as a business or residence. They need to build a structure that will be suitable and safe for its intended function. For example, having proper insulation around pipes so they don't freeze in winter, or using nonflammable materials whenever possible.

It's always a good idea to start out with broad general knowledge of a trade, but many people decide to specialize. Some may prefer to work on heavy construction or roofs, while others prefer to build the interior walls and stairs. Cabinetry and countertops is another specialty.

SOME OF THE OLDEST WOODEN BUILDINGS IN EXISTENCE

SANTA MARÍA DE LORETO DE ACHAO Chile, UNESCO World Heritage Site	Wooden church, circa 1730. Many of its joints are fastened with wooden pegs.
FAIRBANKS HOUSE Dedham, MA	Wooden house dated by dendrochronology to 1641, considered the oldest timber frame structure in North America.
STÅLEKLEIVLOFTET Vindlaus, Norway	Wooden storehouse, circa 1300. Currently used as a museum.
ROYKSTOVAN IN KIRKJUBØ Faroe Islands	Farmhouse, circa 11th century. One of the world's oldest inhabited timber houses.
GREENSTED CHURCH Essex, England	Considered the oldest timber church in the world, circa 998. The churchyard contains the grave of a 12th century crusader.

NANCHAN TEMPLE Shan Xi Sheng, China	Buddhist temple, circa 782. In 1961, the Chinese government recognized it as the oldest standing timber frame building in the country. In 1966, it was destroyed by earthquake, then rebuilt piece by piece.
HORYUJI TEMPLE Nara, Japan, UNESCO World Heritage Site	Temple, circa 607. Considered the oldest wooden building in the world.

HOW DID IT START?

People have relied on carpentry skills for centuries. The word carpenter comes from the ancient Romans. Skilled woodworkers, known as carpentarii (Latin for "chariot makers"), traveled with the Roman army. They built and repaired chariots, wagons, and other wooden supplies. They also built forts, outposts, and shelters for the soldiers. Sometimes they even built bridges the army used to cross rivers. Some of their tools were very similar to their modern counterparts—hammers and nails, saws, and rulers.

Many of the techniques used by modern carpenters are based on those invented centuries ago, in the Middle Ages. The tools used by carpenters back then—such as axes, hammers, and saws—are the same tools that modern-day carpenters use. Some medieval carpenters, commonly called joiners, developed carpentry methods that didn't require nails. Joinery involves fitting pieces of wood together to form a joint. It's most often seen on fine furniture. Look at a wooden drawer. If the pieces are attached by fitting together edges cut like jigsaw puzzle pieces, rather than being nailed or glued, you're looking at joinery. These methods are still used today, although joiners are now commonly called finish carpenters.

Although today's carpentry is often much the same as the carpentry practiced hundreds of years ago, advances in technology and techniques have allowed carpenters to perform their jobs more efficiently. Carpenters today still use hammers and handsaws, but they also use circular saws, nail guns, and table saws to make their jobs easier and to do more precise work. Building materials have also changed. Carpenters still work with wood, but they work with modern building materials such as fiberglass, plastic, and drywall.

Since today's consumers want homes that are more energy efficient and "greener," carpenters

Someone who works on antique furniture or in older buildings might prefer vintage hand tools.

need to be familiar with different types of insulation. Home buyers might also be concerned that the wood in their new home comes from a sustainable forest and that any synthetics used were manufactured without causing undue pollution.

Many different kinds of carpenters may work together on a modern construction site alongside dozens of other professionals such as crane operators, electricians, foremen, plumbers, and welders. Some carpenters specialize in a specific type of work, and others tackle a wide range of carpentry projects every day. No matter what the job is, today's carpenters have their work cut out for them!

WHAT'S IN YOUR TOOLBOX?

Carpenters generally own their own tools. Hammers, nails, pry bars, and tape measures are timeless components of any toolbox. You can find them in all sorts of hardware and home improvement stores. Other items might vary, depending on a particular person's specialty.

A carpenter who builds or restores wooden furniture or renovates historic buildings might prefer vintage tools such as planes or chisels. They might need to acquire them from specialty vendors online or by searching through roadside antique shops.

Someone who works on modern construction sites might prefer power tools. Nail guns are more popular with roofers than hammers, and power saws and drills are a must for large building projects.

Personal Protective Equipment (PPE) is a must for anyone in a construction trade. At a minimum, every carpenter should carry gloves, safety glasses, dust masks, and ear plugs or noise-cancelling earmuffs. The use of other gear might be dictated for heavy power tools or material such as fiberglass insulation.

This carpenter is using a circular saw. He's wearing heavy gloves to protect his hands and safety glasses to keep sawdust and flying particles out of his eyes.

THE BASICS

Carpenters must be good with tools and understand modern building techniques. They need to be aware of their surroundings and other people working around them. They must also be able to adapt to any situation with the tools and skills available to them. These are the skills and techniques that people learn while training to become a carpenter. Some skills, however, are more basic and are sometimes overlooked. These skills and personality traits can greatly help carpenters excel at their craft.

KEEPING FIT

Carpentry is definitely a "hands-on" profession. It helps to be physically fit in a career where much of the working day may be spent lifting lumber or swinging a hammer. Physical fitness can also help reduce the chances of accidents and injuries, especially in dangerous environments. People who are considering a career as a carpenter may want to join a gym or play a sport in their free time. If possible, they should take a class on safe lifting techniques. Working on a busy job site will also help a carpenter stay in shape.

COMMUNICATION SKILLS

Being able to communicate clearly with others is an important trait for carpenters. On a job site, carpenters are in frequent contact with many other types of workers. They need to be able to listen attentively to instructions, give clear directions, and answer questions. They also often must read and create building designs called blueprints. Some may be required to write reports or business letters, or they might be in frequent contact with the customer who hired them for the job.

In an area where a language other than English is common, it's a good idea to learn at least the basics. Carpentry and construction vocabulary in Spanish and Mandarin Chinese is readily available online.

Blueprints are generally drawn up by architects, but carpenters need to know how to read them. Blueprints contain the plan or pattern for the building. They also include important information such as where electrical and plumbing fixtures need to go.

FACTS AND FIGURES

Carpenters frequently use math skills in the course of their workday. They need math skills for making measurements, estimating the materials needed to finish a job, and much more. An independent contractor might need to know how to figure estimates and invoices for clients, as well as payroll.

Carpenters must often add and subtract fractions and decimals. They must also have a good grasp of geometric applications. It's good to be a quick carpenter, but precision and care while measuring is far more important. This is reflected in the carpenter's adage: Measure twice, cut once. In many cases, if a carpenter's measurements are off by just one-sixteenth of an inch, the quality of the project will suffer. Cabinets that can't open and staircases without enough space for people to walk might make for funny online memes, but no one on the building site will be laughing.

This ladder is too big for one person to carry safely. With two people carrying it, neither one of them gets hurt and the ladder is under control so it doesn't swing around and hurt anyone else.

SAFETY FIRST

Like any construction trade, carpentry can be dangerous if people are careless. Carpenters always need to be aware of their surroundings. They need to know where the floor they're standing on ends, be careful not to stand where anything could fall on them, and always wear a hardhat on a construction site.

When using power tools, they need to be sure the cord and plug are in good condition so they don't get an electrical shock—or start a fire. Workers need to unplug power tools if they leave them unattended, and users must be mindful that a cord isn't stretched across where other people need to walk.

Carpenters need to be alert when using products that might create fumes, such as varnish or solvents. They must read all the warnings on the package and use appropriate PPE. They need to practice safe lifting techniques so they don't hurt themselves or anyone else.

BOB VILA

Bob Vila is a TV personality and home improvement expert. He hosted 234 episodes of PBS's long-running home improvement classic *This Old House*. He also hosted three shows of his own—*Bob Vila's Home Again*, *Bob Vila*, and *Restore America with Bob Vila*. He's run his own residential remodeling business and written multiple books about building, renovations, and famous homes. He's also worked with the Peace Corps, Habitat for Humanity, and the National Alliance to End Homelessness.

Currently, he has a website, BobVila.com, which features product reviews, coupons, and do-it-yourself home improvement advice.

CHAPTER TWO

HIGH SCHOOL AND BEYOND

There was a time when vocational classes, such as shop, were common in American high schools. A high school diploma prepared students for their first job in trades such as carpentry or auto mechanics. Lately, however, shop programs are disappearing from school curriculums in favor of purely academic prep for college.

So, if you can't get started on your training in school, where do you start? If you're old enough for working papers, you can get a job at a hardware, home improvement, or lumber store. While you may be restricted to certain tasks if you're younger than 18, you'll get to see lots of different tools and have the chance to ask senior members of the teams all sorts of questions about them.

The Boy Scouts of America offer a merit badge in woodworking. To earn the badge, youngsters must meet the following requirements:

- Demonstrate an understanding of the possible hazards of woodworking.
- Learn about how timber is grown and processed into lumber.

- Demonstrate the proper use, care, and storage of woodworking tools.
- Build something useful from wood they've measured and cut.
- Design and build their own woodworking project.
- Design and build two projects according to different specifications.
- Talk to a carpenter or cabinetmaker about career opportunities and professional benefits.

The exact requirements are available online. So even if you're not a scout, you can work through them on your own or with a parent.

You should also consider taking a first aid class. No matter how careful you are, carpentry involves sharp tools, occasional flying debris, and other hazards.

Working in a big box home improvement store will expose you to a wide variety of tools and building materials.

A neighborhood hardware store will have a smaller selection of merchandise, but the proprietor can probably tell you a lot more about the items they carry.

BEYOND SHOP CLASS

Doing well in high school is the first step toward attaining a career in carpentry. If your school district still offers shop class, that's a great place to start. But even if you never pick up a tool in a classroom setting, there's still a lot you can do to prepare for your chosen career.

Carpenters need to excel in math. When planning a project, they need to be able to figure out how much lumber and other supplies they need, and how much it will cost. They need a thorough understanding of geometry to visualize what a structure will look like when it's built. If they plan to go into business for themselves, they need to know how to estimate the cost of a project and how to bill a customer.

They need a solid background in science. Physics is useful for understanding how forces interreact and how structures remain upright. Chemistry is helpful because a carpenter will use substances such as glues and varnishes.

See what art classes are offered in your school. An art appreciation class that includes some of the world's great architecture could be useful. So would drawing classes. Although buildings tend to be designed by architects, there are plenty of other projects that will require you to draw plans.

Good language arts skills are essential. You'll need to be able to give clear instructions to your work crew, draft project proposals, and give updates on the status of projects. If you go into business for yourself, you'll need to maintain professional social media accounts to attract customers.

Computer skills are invaluable in any trade, and any basic business classes are worth investigating. If there's a language other than English commonly spoken in your area, it's good to have at least a basic understanding. And of course, PE, because carpentry is a very physical profession.

As you can see, there are plenty of skills you can acquire in high school to set you up for the next step on your educational journey.

CAREER AND TECHNICAL EDUCATION

Some teens are fortunate enough to attend schools that offer Career and Technical Education (CTE). CTE programs can prepare young people for a job, or for the higher education needed for a particular career. They're aimed at preparing students for skilled jobs that can earn a comfortable wage with an associate's degree or certificate, rather than a four-year college degree, with its associated burden of student debt.

President Donald Trump signed the Strengthening Career and Technical Education for the 21st Century act into law in 2018. It allocates funds for CTE programs at the high school level. CTE programs offer a variety of career clusters, including construction trades.

Career Connections is a program created by the Carpenters International Training Fund (CITF) High school educators are provided with materials created in union training centers and supported by union carpenters.

This young woman is using a plane in a wood shop. You can see she's wearing safety glasses to protect her eyes and working on a flat, steady surface.

A CONVERSATION WITH A CARPENTER

Here are some insights from Greg Moskal, an educator with a lifetime of experience with the art and craft of carpentry.

How did you first get involved with carpentry?

Carpentry was a big part of my life growing up. My family built our home, a log cabin, when I was 10. After high school, I got a summer carpentry job with a small outfit. I learned a great deal through one-on-one instruction. I had the opportunity to do many different types of jobs—from small home repairs to building entire houses from start to finish.

Besides teaching, how do you make use of your carpentry skills?

I use my carpentry skills to generate a supplemental income. There is always an opportunity for work. Through networking, I have had the opportunity to help build the homes of some traditional artisans. These people are extremely skilled in traditional joinery where the building frame is held together without a single nail. I have worked with other trained carpenters on timber frame barn restorations and furniture. I repair my own home, which would otherwise be very costly. I also find great enjoyment [in] making furniture and crafts.

What advice would you give to youths interested in pursuing a career in carpentry?

Start with basic technology classes. Technical drawing is a must for people who want to become carpenters. See if your high school has basic woodworking, carpentry, and residential structure classes. For more in-depth knowledge, students can look into local vocational schools. Students can also look for summer work with a local contractor. Small-time contractors usually give the broadest exposure to different aspects of carpentry and building. Larger firms offer more specialized carpentry. Students may also have a family member or friend who would be willing to mentor them.

AFTER HIGH SCHOOL

Beyond high school, there are several ways to pursue an education in carpentry. Some people go on to become successful carpenters without any kind of formal education at all, but it is rare. In today's world, a degree or certificate of training is much more attractive to potential employers than experience alone.

Carpenters need technical skills, such as knowing how to read blueprints. They must also be familiar with building codes. In addition, all carpenters must pass the Occupational Safety and Health Administration's (OSHA) 10-hour safety course.

TRADE SCHOOLS

Vocational schools (also called trade schools) teach a wide range of career skills, including carpentry. Some vocational schools accept students at 16 years of age. Others require a General Educational Development (GED) or high school diploma. The main purpose of a trade school is to train students for a career, or vocation. Trade schools can be an invaluable resource for young men and women who want to secure a future in the world of carpentry.

Students don't need a carpentry background to enroll in a trade school, but they do need to select the type of training they want to pursue. For example, a student may decide to pursue a residential or commercial carpentry degree. Residential carpentry courses focus on the skills required to build homes, such as drywall installation and roofing. In commercial carpentry courses, students might learn how to install suspended ceilings and office cubicles. It should be mentioned that, outside of school, probably the best way to secure a carpentry career is to become an apprentice. Hands-on work with a trained expert is the most efficient way to sharpen your skills and learn about the profession. Many vocational schools and colleges offer apprenticeship programs, as do carpentry unions.

According to TradeCollege.org, carpentry is the 38th most popular major in New York state, with 36 degrees and certificates awarded in the 2020-21 academic year.

GETTING A COLLEGE DEGREE

Colleges across the United States offer carpentry degrees. The required coursework for these degrees is often very similar to what one would receive in a trade school. In fact, some trade schools have begun to offer college degrees in addition to job training.

To earn a college degree, students are usually expected to take courses in different subjects such as English composition, math, and psychology. Many of these courses can be very useful to someone who desires a career in carpentry. A college degree is also helpful in case you decide to change careers later in life.

Colleges may also offer courses on modern, cutting-edge topics that might not be part of a trade school's curriculum, such as classes about environmental issues or green building design. Although college can be a financial burden for many people, there are scholarships and grants available for people who need them.

Some scholarships are specifically intended for carpentry students. For example, in 2023, the Home Depot Foundation announced a $200,000 investment in scholarships for women pursuing degrees in the construction trades. A Path to Pro for Women scholarship provides $4,000 in financial assistance to a qualified female student. The Foundation has pledged $50 million overall to Path to Pro programs that assist students, military veterans, and underserved communities.

HOW DO YOU KNOW IF YOU'VE GOT THE RIGHT STUFF?

The Bureau of Labor Statistics (BLS) recommends the following personality traits and skillsets for people considering a career in carpentry:

BUSINESS SKILLS	Carpenters who opt to run their own business are responsible for billing, inventory, and possibly payroll.
DETAIL ORIENTED	"Measure twice, cut once" is a way of life for carpenters. They need to be able to measure accurately and follow complex, detailed instructions.
DEXTERITY	Carpentry is a hands-on trade
INTERPERSONAL SKILLS	Carpenters need to be able to work with a construction crew and communicate effectively with customers.
MATH SKILLS	Carpenters need geometry and trigonometry to figure interior and exterior spaces of a structure. They also need business math skills for billing customers and ordering supplies.
PHYSICAL STRENGTH	Carpenters lift timber and use heavy tools.
PROBLEM-SOLVING SKILLS	Projects often need to be adjusted "on the fly" in response to supply issues, customer requests, and other unforeseen circumstances.
READING COMPREHENSION	Carpenters need to follow detailed instructions. They need to understand safety warnings on power tools and chemicals they use.

Architects, carpenters, and contractors often draw blueprints on a computer these days. This is one of many reasons why carpenters need up-to-date computer skills.

COMPLETING AN INTERNSHIP

Before earning a degree in carpentry, students might be expected to complete an internship. Internships help students make the transition from college life to the working world. Although interns are usually not paid for their work, they benefit by working with experienced professionals in successful businesses. Internships are sometimes listed on job-finding websites such as Indeed. Home Depot's Path to Pro website also features a section for finding jobs.

This is one of the best ways for a college student with little professional experience to learn carpentry skills. Internships are generally shorter and more informal than apprenticeships, and some internships can count for college credit. Another great benefit to internships is that the companies that offer internships sometimes hire the people they've trained after graduation.

WHAT ELSE?

Some people don't end up going to college. Instead, they travel, do volunteer work, or find a permanent job. College is a major expense and sometimes it's better to take some time and examine all the options before deciding what to do. Getting a college education is always a big help when it comes to advancing one's career, but it is not the only option. Luckily, high school graduates who choose not to attend college have many choices when it comes to their future.

Armed forces construction specialists work around the globe. They build and maintain structures on military bases, and provide disaster relief and recovery to civilians.

THE ARMED FORCES

Many young people choose to enter the military or the military reserves after graduation. Just as in the civilian world, carpenters are needed in the military. After basic military training, recruits interested in carpentry receive specialized training. Upon being discharged from the military, veterans can apply the training they received to their carpentry career. Receiving training through the armed forces eliminates the prospect of student loan debt.

The Army offers a career path as a Carpentry and Masonry Specialist. This path is open to active duty personal as well as reservists and members of the National Guard. It requires a score of 88 in the General Maintenance (GM) category of the Armed Services Vocational Aptitude Battery (ASVAB).

The Air Force offers a career path as a Structural Specialist. Personnel in this program are responsible for building and maintaining all sorts of structures. The ASVAB Mechanical section is a prerequisite for the program.

Construction Battalions in the U.S. Navy are referred to as "Seabees" (CBs). This is short for "Construction Battalions." Active-duty enlisted personnel as well as reservists are eligible to serve in the Seabees.

JOINING THE JOB CORPS

The Job Corps is a vocational training program for young people ages 16 to 24. It's managed by the U.S. Department of Labor. This program gives youths from low-income families a chance to be trained in a wide range of vocations, including carpentry. The Job Corps also offers tutoring programs for students who want to earn their diploma or GED, provides mentoring programs, and helps its participants create solid résumés. Although not everyone can attend the Job Corps, it provides many with valuable vocational training. The program is free for those who qualify.

Students in the carpentry program can earn a pre-apprenticeship certificate, OSHA safety certification, and other professional certifications. The Job Corps can help students connect with military recruiters if that's a good fit for them to continue their education. They also work in partnership with business owners to help graduates find their first jobs.

Volunteers from Habitat for Humanity build homes for people in need. They also assist in disaster recovery, as in the aftermath of Hurricane Katrina, when many homes were damaged or destroyed.

SERVING THE COMMUNITY

Some volunteer programs also offer people the opportunity to learn carpentry. By volunteering for a nonprofit organization such as Habitat for Humanity, which builds and restores homes for families in need of shelter around the world, young people can learn valuable carpentry skills while assessing if this career is right for them.

Job search websites such as LinkedIn and Indeed often list volunteer opportunities. Be sure to read the requirements carefully.

The Peace Corps also offers people the opportunity to volunteer their carpentry skills for a good cause. However, the organization expects applicants to already have some experience in the field. Along with proper carpentry training and certification, the experience that a person gains while volunteering can help him or her climb the career ladder.

PRESIDENT CARTER AND HABITAT FOR HUMANITY

Jimmy Carter served as the 39th president of the United States from 1977 to 1981. Although his tenure in the White House saw many turbulent world events, today he's best remembered and honored as a humanitarian.

Habitat for Humanity International (HFHI) is a nonprofit organization founded in 1976. Its mission is to provide decent housing to families in need. Volunteers build new homes and help repair houses damaged in major disasters. HFHI received global attention when Jimmy Carter and former First Lady Rosalynn Carter began working on projects with the organization in 1984. For 35 years—until Jimmy Carter was in his 90s—they worked directly on building sites with other Habitat volunteers around the world.

In 1982, he founded the Carter Center, an organization devoted to promoting peace and human rights. In 2002, Jimmy Carter was awarded the Nobel Peace Prize.

President Carter didn't just serve as a figurehead or donor. For decades he worked on Habitat for Humanity projects alongside volunteers from all walks of life.

REMOTE LEARNING

Finally, some people seek training from online courses. This can be a good way to learn about carpentry, but it also has certain drawbacks. For instance, not all online courses offer national certification. Students who participate in an online course may require additional steps to become licensed or certified. Certified carpenters have received up-to-date instruction from an officially recognized training organization, and they have the certificate to prove it. Some training programs offer national certification, while others offer certification based on a particular state or region.

Although the COVID-19 pandemic showed us that many things can be learned online, carpentry involves manual skills. People who learn online also won't receive hands-on training, which is the best way to learn when it comes to carpentry. Anyone who is thinking of signing up for an online course should be sure he or she understands exactly what the course offers. In addition, students studying remotely would likely have to provide their own tools, supplies, safety equipment, and suitable workspace. A kitchen table is fine for setting up a laptop, but it's not a good place to saw or hammer nails. Remote learning might be a good choice for someone who's refreshing their credentials, but a new student is probably better off in an in-person learning environment.

MENTORSHIP

A mentor is an expert in a particular field who serves as a coach to someone just learning or starting out.

It's not uncommon for someone's first mentor to be a family member, such as a grandparent teaching them basic skills in a basement workshop. In addition to passing along skills and the love of a craft, this type of mentor might encourage someone to seek out more advanced instruction or pursue professional credentials.

In a professional environment, a mentor might be a master craftsman or a more senior member of a union. This type of mentor will be able to share useful knowledge about the business side of the craft and how to progress through the union ranks, as well as sophisticated craft techniques they've perfected. Both types of mentors are valuable. A family member's encouragement can get someone started on a career path they'll love. A professional mentor can help them thrive in the current business world.

Learning a craft from a family member is a great way to get started.

CHAPTER THREE

PROFESSIONAL TRAINING AND CREDENTIALS

Part of the appeal of a career in carpentry is that it doesn't require the years of college and extensive student loan debt required for many other careers. But without a fancy degree or title, how will people know you're qualified?

The answer is professional certification. Professional certification as a carpenter is achieved via an apprenticeship in the United Brotherhood of Carpenters and Joiners (UBC). Those interested in a career in the construction trades may choose to certify as a carpenter, covering all aspects of construction, or choose a specialty such as millwright, pile driver, cabinetmaker, or floor coverer. In addition, all carpenters are required to pass an OSHA safety program. Some carpenters may choose to pursue further certification through specialist organizations such as the National Association of the Remodeling Industry (NARI) or the National Wood Flooring Association (NWFA).

The UBC is one of the largest labor unions. They also represent workers in Canada. This is their facility in London, Ontario.

BECOMING AN APPRENTICE

Carpenters learned their craft through apprenticeship for centuries, long before universities taught carpentry courses. Apprenticeship is a method of training that generally combines hands-on, worksite experience with classroom instruction. Many professionals will say the best way to become a carpenter is to apprentice with an experienced journeyperson or journeyworker. (The term journeyman is outdated and noninclusive. Journeyperson or journeyworker are more common now.)

Journeypersons have completed an apprenticeship program and have become certified carpenters. They pass on the skills, techniques, and knowledge they have accumulated during their career to their apprentices. A journeyperson makes sure that his or her apprentice spends time on many different tasks on the work site. In this way, the apprentice gains valuable experience and a well-rounded education.

Another great benefit of apprenticeships is that the trainee can earn a salary while being trained. For example, apprentices in one of the Carpenters Training Institute's (CTI) programs can expect to earn about $33,000 per year while training. Most college internships do not pay a salary, which can make it difficult for young people trying to start a career. Many students with internships need to get an additional job or two to pay their living expenses. With an apprenticeship, however, students are often paid for their work. The beginning pay is usually only about half of what a journeyperson makes, but the pay goes up as the apprentice gains knowledge and experience. In some cases, apprentices may also receive health benefits.

THE HISTORY OF APPRENTICESHIP

The concept of formal apprenticeship dates back at least as far as the trade guilds of medieval Europe. Members of a trade who lived in the same town banded together to form a guild. They set the standards for workmanship and prices in that trade and offered mutual aid to guild members, their widows, and orphans. Workers not associated with the guild weren't allowed to practice that trade in the town.

Shops were owned by master craftsmen. They would accept apprentices for training, usually for a period of seven years. They would feed, clothe, and house apprentices, in addition to teaching them their craft. The apprentice's parents paid the master for training their child. If an apprentice ran away before completing their training, the master could have them caught and returned, much like runaway indentured servants or enslaved people.

At the end of their training, an apprentice would receive their own set of tools and become a journeyperson. This meant that they could work their trade for day wages. They might continue to work for the same master, perhaps overseeing other apprentices. Or they could work for others, giving their master's name as reference. After a set amount of time, a journeyperson would be considered a master craftsman in their own right and be allowed to open their own shop.

This system was brought to North America and practiced in the colonies. Eventually the system of apprenticeship died out as college education, rather than training with a master, became the accepted path to professional success. Many jobs that were once performed by master craftsmen, such as weaving, became automated. Business owners were able to hire untrained labor to work in factories, instead of paying for craftsmanship.

Today, re-enactors practice medieval woodwork with traditional tools.

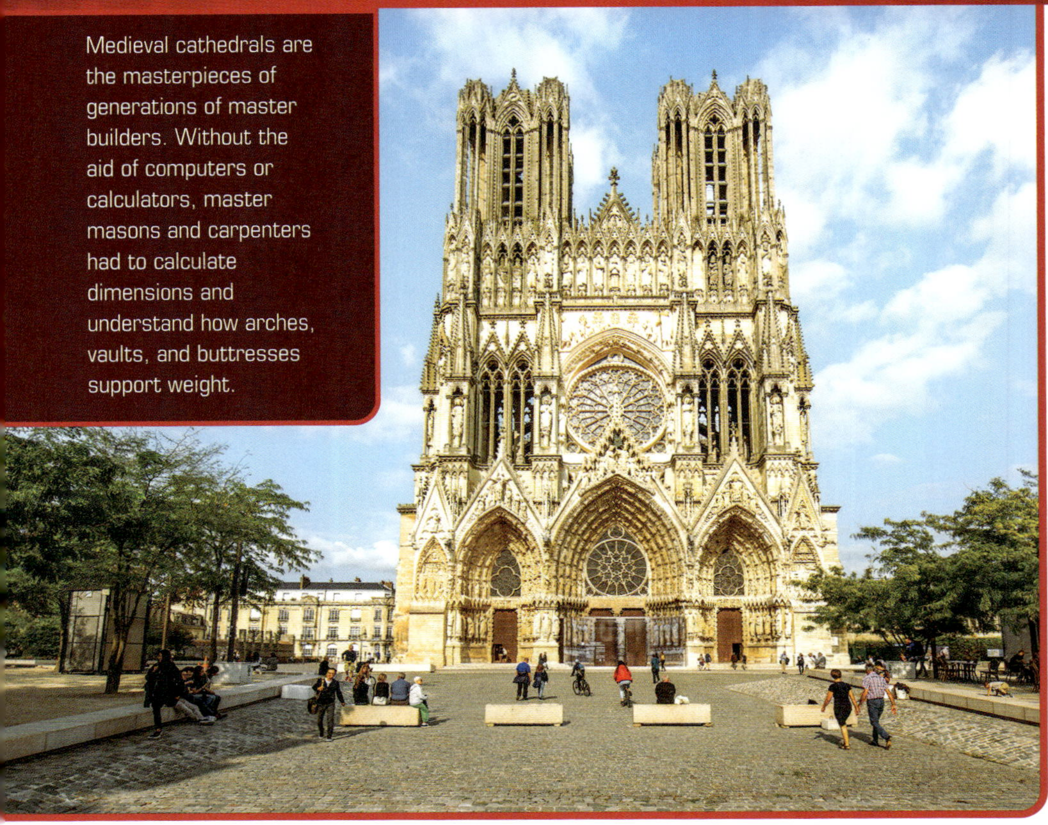

Medieval cathedrals are the masterpieces of generations of master builders. Without the aid of computers or calculators, master masons and carpenters had to calculate dimensions and understand how arches, vaults, and buttresses support weight.

MODERN APPRENTICESHIP

Most modern apprenticeship programs last for four years, or about the same time it would take to receive a bachelor's degree in college. However, it's possible for some apprentices to finish a program in less time, particularly if they received training in the armed forces or have another form of experience.

Carpentry apprenticeships cover a wide range of specialties, such as rough carpentry, cabinetmaking, shipbuilding, acoustical tile installation, and stage and prop creation. Unlike apprenticeships of the past, modern apprenticeships often include classroom instruction. Required class work may include courses in mathematics, geometry, and mechanics, among other basic courses.

At the current time, completing a carpentry apprenticeship requires about 4 years, 7,000 hours of on-the-job training (OJT), and 640 hours of classroom work.

PRE-APPRENTICESHIP

In most states, you must be 17 before you can become an apprentice. In some states, you must be 18. Pre-apprenticeship programs are often much like classes offered in vocational schools; in fact, many trade schools offer this type of program, as do some high schools. A pre-apprenticeship simply prepares someone for an apprenticeship and increases the chances of being accepted before other people who are the same age but have less experience because they have not been through such a program.

The Job Corps, mentioned in the previous chapter, is sometimes considered a pre-apprenticeship program. Military construction training is also considered a pre-apprenticeship. Home Depot's Path to Pro Youth and High School programs feature a Pre-Apprenticeship Certification Training (PACT). For more information about pre-apprenticeship programs, contact your local carpenters union.

It's possible to make it without being an apprentice first, but it may not be easy. Being a competent worker with solid experience helps, but it's not always enough. Most organizations that employ teams of carpenters—particularly commercial and residential construction firms—will require the certification that results from an apprenticeship program.

Uncertified carpenters might be lucky enough to land a job with a small local business, especially if they know someone who can help them out. Some carpenters start their own private businesses and do very well. However, it still usually takes years of fieldwork to gain the expertise required to run a private carpentry business.

COMPLETING AN APPRENTICESHIP

In partnership with the UBC, the Carpenters Training Institute offers apprenticeships in five major disciplines. Apprentices earn approximately $33,000 to $46,000 per year, plus benefits, during training. Each apprenticeship requires four years, 7,000 hours of OJT, and at least 640 classroom hours. Upon completion of their apprenticeship, journeypersons might make $60,000 to $84,000 per year, plus benefits. A journeyperson might continue their education and eventually become certified as a foreman or superintendent.

CARPENTERS learn all facets of constructing a building from blueprints to finished structure. They use a variety of equipment from basic hand tools to computers. Carpenters may be involved in both heavy outdoor construction work and more detailed interior projects.

MILLWRIGHTS install precision equipment in facilities such as factories, breweries, and mills. They use everything from hand tools to micrometers. This apprenticeship requires 800 hours of classroom study.

PILE DRIVERS utilize heavy equipment to excavate building sites and lay foundations. This is precision work because the foundation supports the entire structure. This is heavy outdoor construction work.

FLOOR COVERERS learn to measure and install all sorts of floor coverings, from hardwood to carpet. They must also complete the International Standards & Training Alliance (INSTALL) certification program.

CABINETMAKERS create custom woodwork for structures. This includes trim moldings, mantels—and yes, cabinets. They might also fabricate furniture or store fixtures. This is highly detailed, indoor work that will be in full view of people utilizing the building.

UNIONS

Most apprenticeships are offered by carpentry unions—in fact, when someone begins an apprenticeship, he or she will probably be expected to join the local union. For example, an aspiring carpenter in western New York would join the Western New York Carpenters Local 276, which has offices in Buffalo and Rochester. All regional carpentry unions are members of the UBC.

A union is an organization of workers within a specific profession. There are unions for carpenters, electricians, clothing manufacturers, bakers, musicians, teachers, actors, writers, and many other professions. Unions are important and powerful organizations designed to uphold the rights of workers. The rise of industrialization reduced the importance of the old trade and craft guilds. Businesses turned to unskilled labor to produce products. Prior to the existence of unions in the United States, workers had little or no rights in the workplace. Most workers—skilled and unskilled—were paid very little, worked under very dangerous conditions, had no benefits, and had no say in how business was conducted. The establishment of unions gave workers a voice in the workplace.

Union members are expected to pay dues to fund union activities. This often includes a fund to pay workers if they participate in a strike. The benefits of joining a union are often well worth the cost. In addition to bargaining for excellent health benefits, fair working hours, and pay raises, carpentry unions offer the best training available. It takes 8,000 hours, or about four years, to finish the union apprenticeship program. Completion of the program results in national accreditation.

A strike is the ultimate union negotiating tool. If a settlement can't be reached another way, union members will stop working until a new contract is negotiated.

THE UNITED BROTHERHOOD OF CARPENTERS AND JOINERS OF AMERICA

The UBC is one of the largest building trades unions in North America. It represents more than half a million workers in the United States and Canada.

Workers founded the UBC in Chicago in 1881 at a convention of 36 carpenters from 11 cities. Canadian carpenters soon joined the fledgling union. Membership exploded from an initial 2,042 to more than 50,000 by the turn of the century.

The UBC's first general secretary was Peter J. McGuire, a prominent labor leader. McGuire had experienced working long hours for poor pay and wanted to improve conditions for workers. Since its inception, the UBC has championed causes such as the uniform workday and workweek, safe working conditions, and fair wages.

Today, membership has expanded to include other building trades. The UBC offers professional certification via apprenticeship in five major construction disciplines, as well as additional training in a multitude of specialties.

The UBC is one of a few major unions that doesn't fall under the umbrella of the American Federation of Labor and the Congress of Industrial Organizations (AFL-CIO).

Today, Labor Day is generally recognized as the end of summer and beginning of the new school year. Its original meaning—honoring workers—has become lost over time. Peter J. McGuire, founder of the UBC, is credited with the idea of making Labor Day a national holiday.

CARPENTERS IN THE ENTERTAINMENT INDUSTRY

Carpenters are an indispensable part of the entertainment industry. They work in theaters, films, and live events. They do everything from constructing an entire life-sized Hobbit village for the *Lord of the Rings* films to building a safe and functional stage for your favorite rock band.

Carpenters in the entertainment industry are represented by the International Alliance of Stage Employees, Moving Picture Technicians, Artists and Allied Crafts of the United States, Its Territories and Canada (IATSE).

Workers formed the IATSE in 1893. Today it represents 168,000 workers in Canada and the United States via 362 local unions. It provides continuing education in safety and craft skills for members. The union also champions diversity and tolerance in the workplace and strives to make the entertainment industry "greener" and more sustainable.

Carpenters and scenic designers constructed a life-sized version of Hobbiton in New Zealand for the *Lord of the Rings* films. Today, the sets used for *The Hobbit* trilogy remain as a permanent tourist attraction.

PROFESSIONAL CERTIFICATION

Once a carpenter completes their union apprenticeship, they're ready to begin their career as a journeyperson. This means they've earned their certification as a carpenter, millwright, cabinet maker, floor coverer, or pile driver. The UBC offers training in many more construction crafts including things such as scaffolding and welding, for those who want to specialize in construction, as well as acoustical ceilings and stair building, for those who prefer interior work. There are also programs in green building awareness and solar installation.

A UBC carpenter's training is accessible through their Training Verification Card (TVC). This is a wallet card printed with a QR code. When scanned, the card provides the carpenter's union status and all their current certifications. Each new certification is uploaded to a central database upon completion. Unlike a traditional CV or résumé, a TVC is always up to date.

In addition to the traditional apprenticeship programs, UBC offers special programs for transitioning military veterans. These programs are a fast-track for vets with construction experience to obtain their civilian certifications as carpenters or millwrights.

Once a carpenter earns their certification, they need to find a job. It's possible they may stay on at the project they worked on as an apprentice. They can also check out their local union website or a job posting website such as Indeed or ZipRecruiter.

CHAPTER FOUR

GETTING STARTED

Looking for your first job can be a combination of exciting and terrifying. It's exciting to contemplate the independence that comes with earning your own paycheck. If you're uncomfortable talking about yourself, the prospect can be daunting. Luckily, there are resources available to help you succeed in your job hunt.

THE JOB HUNT

Places such as libraries and community centers often offer free classes on résumé writing and interview skills. If you're a student in a vocational training program, your school might have a person or department to help with job placement.

It's helpful to know what your career goals are. Perhaps you've known since you were 10 that you want to join your uncle's business and build houses. Maybe you have general carpentry training, and you'd like to try a few things before continuing your education. Or perhaps you have a goal in mind that you know requires special training, such as working in the entertainment industry.

The internet is your friend when it comes to searching for a job. Sites such as Indeed let you specify a geographic area, as well as search for internships or apprenticeships. On LinkedIn, you can search for jobs and also follow organizations that interest you, such as unions or companies. Your local union website may have a job page. If you're looking for day work to get some experience, there are websites where you can post your information and people hire you for a specific task. You can also check the bulletin boards at hardware stores and lumber yards.

Before starting your job search, gather all the information you'll need. Be sure to have your working papers if needed. You'll need your Social Security card and driver's license (if you have one). If you're certified in first aid or CPR, have those cards handy.

Employers usually ask for references—people they can call or email to learn more about you. Often, they specify people outside of your household. If you've worked before, you'll be asked to list your employers, the dates you worked, and why you left, along with contact information. If you expect to fill out an application, you should have this information neatly printed, or saved on a document on your phone so you can easily copy it. (Pro tip: even if you filled out an application or uploaded a résumé online, you may still be asked to fill out a paper application. Have all the information you'll need readily available.)

Many cities have career centers that can help you find a job or free career development workshops in your area. You can usually find this information on your state's Department of Labor website.

NEW YORK STATE OF OPPORTUNITY. | Department of Labor

FACTS & FIGURES FROM THE BLS

Here are some interesting figures from the BLS compiled with data collected between 2003 and 2020.

- One in ten construction industry workers, or about 1.2 million, are women.
- About 30% of construction industry workers are Hispanic, versus 17% of the total employed population.
- Most construction industry workers—about 60%—are white. They are more likely to be union members.
- Union members earn higher wages than nonunion workers.
- About one in five construction industry workers are in business, management, or financial positions.
- One in four construction industry workers are foreign born. They don't earn as much as native-born workers.
- Construction industry workers are less likely to have attended college.
- About one in four construction industry workers are self-employed.

BUILDING YOUR NETWORK

Networking is something most people participate in every day, via social media. You've probably got a variety of friends or followers on different accounts, most likely a combination of family and friends you know in real life, and online buddies who share common interests.

When you begin your career, you need to collect and organize social and business contacts to create business opportunities. The purpose of this network is to form a collection of people that can be called upon when the need arises.

For professional purposes, you should probably set up separate social media accounts. Use your full name and profession—something like "Jane Smith, Certified Carpenter" works fine. It's okay if some of your friends or family follow your new accounts—just don't fill them with memes or wild party pictures. Keep the content clean and professional. Post about your latest project (even if it's something you did just for fun), pictures of interesting buildings, or industry-related books you've read. Follow other contractors, carpenters, hardware retailers, and lumber yards.

Don't forget in-person networking! Any event hosted by your union, whether it's a social event or a volunteer opportunity, is a great way to connect with other industry professionals.

LinkedIn is a social media platform designed for business networking. Your profile page is designed to be an online résumé. Many large construction-related businesses and organizations have profiles you can follow. You can also search for and apply to jobs online.

Facebook is probably the social media platform you're most familiar with. It's very flexible—you can post pictures and videos as well as text and send private messages. Most businesses have a presence on Facebook.

Instagram and Pinterest are good platforms to share portfolios of photographs. Someone who specializes in furniture, cabinetry, or interiors might use these platforms. Or you could use them to document a big project through a series of photos.

YOUR RÉSUMÉ AND COVER LETTER

A résumé is an essential tool for anyone hoping to establish a career after graduation. Since it's the first glimpse an employer will get of a potential worker, a résumé needs to be neat, precise, and informative.

In a nutshell, a good résumé should include relevant educational and professional experiences listed in chronological order on a single sheet of paper. The information on a résumé is generally concise and to the point, and includes the applicant's personal strengths and talents, especially those that an employer would consider to be assets. Your first résumé will include a lot of educational background. Employers understand this. You can list any volunteer experience on a construction project, and any work experience, even in an unrelated field. An employer will be happy to hear from any former supervisor who can vouch for your good work habits.

Some people refer to résumé-writing guides that are available online and at the library when creating their résumé. Word processing programs include several résumé templates to get you started. Others choose to have a professional writer prepare their résumé or enlist the help of a friend or family member with résumé-writing experience.

Besides listing the applicant's education and relevant job experience, a résumé should list any specialized training, apprenticeships, internships, or other experience pertaining to the job the applicant is trying to get. An experienced carpenter might have different résumés depending on the type of carpentry job. For instance, a résumé that is put together with a commercial or residential building job in mind might be different from a résumé aimed at getting a job such as house remodeling, building scaffolding, or another specialty job.

If you don't own a good printer, you can usually print your résumé at a public library for about 10 cents a page. For about double that price, you can have it printed on a top-quality laser printer on heavy paper at an office supply store.

Employers generally expect to receive a cover letter with a résumé. Just as with a résumé, a cover letter should contain very specific information. Writers should begin their cover letter by introducing themselves and stating why they are sending a résumé. The body of the cover letter should highlight educational and professional experience that would make them a good fit for the job. A résumé and cover letter are often sent electronically, but be prepared with good, printed copies when you go for an interview.

Be sure to spellcheck and proofread your résumé, or better yet, have someone else look it over. Print neat copies and carry them in a folder so they don't wrinkle.

LANDING AN INTERVIEW

After getting an employer's attention with a well-written résumé and cover letter, an applicant may be asked to come in for an interview. Not all interviews follow the same format or deal with the same issues. One interview might take place in an office, whereas another might take place on a construction site. No matter where the interview takes place, it is a good idea to follow basic rules of etiquette. Arrive on time, or better yet—a few minutes early. Being courteous and polite to anyone you encounter will greatly improve your chance of landing a job.

Before going on an interview, you should research the company so you can answer any questions related to its business. An applicant should know the name of their interviewer, use it in the interview, and always treat the interviewer with respect. Interviewers want to hear job applicants talk about themselves and reveal their knowledge and expertise. Applicants should maintain eye contact, refrain from fidgeting, and speak clearly.

First impressions count for everything when applying for a job. It's important that job applicants dress well for interviews. Be sure your hair is neat and don't wear heavy fragrances. It's not always necessary to wear a suit, but neat and clean clothes are a must. If the interview is at a construction site, wear suitable shoes or boots—just make sure they're clean! Don't chew gum during the interview. It's also important to shake hands with the interviewer before and after the interview.

Interviewers will often conclude the interview by saying that they will "be in touch," but an applicant should still ask when they might hear from them. This helps show that the applicant is interested in beginning work. Also, it is usually good etiquette to send a follow-up letter several days after the interview, generally via email. Follow-up letters should be short and not too formal. Job seekers shouldn't wait around for an answer from one business before going on their next interview. Going to as many interviews as possible increases your chances of landing a job.

Interviewing for a job is a skill. It's a good idea to practice speaking in front of a mirror or with a friend or family member.

WOMEN IN CARPENTRY

Most people tend to regard carpentry and other construction trades as male professions. And most carpenters are men. However, the idea of a female carpenter isn't a novelty.

Colonial Williamsburg has records of women working in building trades in the 18th century. Today, women interpreters learn historic building trades such as joinery and demonstrate them alongside their male counterparts. They learn their trades as apprentices to one of the master craftsmen on staff, using reproductions of 18th century woodworking tools.

Margaret Ellings was the first woman to join the UBC, in 1935. Today, all carpentry jobs are open to women. In 1998, the UBC organized Sisters in the Brotherhood to encourage more women to train and excel in construction trades.

As of 2020, the BLS estimated that there were 1.2 million women employed in the construction industry, or about one out of every ten workers. To encourage more women to train for construction trades, the Home Depot Foundation recently pledged $200,000 to a scholarship fund for female students.

There's more to modern construction than just brute strength. Anyone with an interest and aptitude can find a place in the industry.

YOU'RE HIRED

After a successful interview, you might be called back for a second interview with the same person or perhaps someone higher up in the organization. Once you are offered a position, your prospective employer will probably run a background check to see if you have a criminal record, and sometimes a credit check. You might still be hired if you have a criminal record, but it's always best to answer such questions truthfully on your initial application rather than have it discovered later. You may be asked to take a drug test, especially if you'll be driving company vehicles or operating heavy equipment, such as cranes.

New hires are generally on probation for the first 90 days of their employment while they become accustomed to the standards expected at their new job. A new hire who displays a pattern of tardiness, absence, or disregard of company rules might be asked to leave before the 90 days are up. During this time, you'll be paid, but won't receive any benefits or paid time off (PTO). In some companies, new hires receive a small raise after their probationary period.

Landing your first job is an amazing feeling, but it's only the first step. You need to keep proving that you're a good fit for the company.

CHAPTER FIVE

YOUR NEW CAREER

One of the joys of a career in carpentry is that there are so many interesting paths to explore. Modern carpentry has expanded to include most building trades. Do you want to build energy-efficient houses? New high-tech professional buildings? How about the safest skyscraper in the world?

Or perhaps you're interested in old-world woodworking skills. You can learn to build furniture or cabinetry by hand or restore old buildings. If you love history, you might consider a position at a living history museum, demonstrating historic woodworking and carpentry.

Perhaps you've always dreamed of working in the theater or on movie sets or even creating immersive worlds at a theme park.

The possibilities for a well-paid and enjoyable career are limited only by your imagination!

ROUGH FRAMER

The first carpenters to work on a job site are usually the rough framers, also called rough carpenters or simply framers. Their job is incredibly important, because if the frame isn't structurally sound, the rest of the building won't be safe. Framers create the support structures for buildings, which requires them to work not only with wood, but also with other types of materials. For instance, many modern wall frames are made of metal beams.

The most common framing jobs involve building the frames for walls, floors, and roofs. These frames form the "skeleton" which the rest of the building is constructed around. Buildings that feature arches or cathedral ceilings require advanced skills to ensure that the frame will properly support the weight of the building.

Framers also build the forms (or molds) used to pour concrete structures, as well as the chutes used to transfer concrete into the forms. Other jobs may include making support structures when building tunnels, replacing rotten wood in old homes, and digging holes for support posts.

Even if a finished structure doesn't appear to be made of wood, there's a good chance the frame looks like this.

A framer constructed the form for this cement. The form needs to be built precisely so that all the pieces fit together properly. If the measurements aren't correct, cement and labor will be wasted making corrections, and that costs extra money.

Rough framers must be able to read blueprints and diagrams and use them to build frameworks, forms, scaffolds, supports, and many other rough structures. They must be quick yet precise when measuring, cutting, and assembling lumber. If the angles and sizes of their frames are not perfect, the materials that are added later will not fit properly. To achieve exact measurements, framers use tape measures, levels, squares, and plumb bobs.

A new framer can gain experience working on a new development, where all the houses are the same. However, building custom homes provide new experiences and challenges.

FINISHER

If a rough carpenter is the first person on a job site, the finisher is one of the last. As the name suggests, finishers put the final touches on a home. Their work begins after the building is constructed and insulated, and after plumbing and electricity have been installed. They build, assemble, and install the decorative elements that make a structure look pleasant and ready to be lived in. The most common finishing jobs are cutting and installing wood trim for doors and windows and molding for walls and floors. These are the pieces that cover rough edges and corners. Finishers are sometimes called trim carpenters.

Cutting molding and trim is precise work. Angles and measurements need to be perfect to ensure that the finished product looks appealing. Some finishers specialize in joinery, a method of fitting wood pieces together without using fasteners such as nails and screws. Depending on the company and the size of the job, a finisher might also install counters, doors, flooring, railings, stairs, and windows. Many finishers restore older homes, making them look new again.

Finishers need to be aware of current trends and styles. They also need to be up to date on "green" initiatives, such as using fast-growing woods like bamboo or sourcing other types of sustainable building materials.

Finishers need to be neat and precise. Their work is out in plain sight!

Today, people don't remodel their kitchen just to make it look good. Often, they want to install new energy- and water-efficient appliances and fixtures.

CABINETMAKER

Cabinetmakers build and repair furniture and cabinets. Sometimes they create objects from scratch; other times they assemble parts that have already been cut and shaped. Cabinetmakers must be good at reading blueprints, diagrams, and instructions. A highly capable cabinetmaker can build a perfect product according to a customer's specifications. Most are very good at repairing broken items as well.

Cabinetmakers work in commercial spaces, too. They might create decorative wall panels for a hotel or office building or cover exposed beams or columns.

In addition to wood, cabinetmakers work with many other materials, such as Formica, glass, and granite. They must know how to cut exact joints so that pieces fit together perfectly. They also use sandpaper, glue, wood stains, paint, and shapers to put finishing touches on the items they make. Besides cabinets, they also make items such as racks, shelves, and tables. Displays and retail sales fixtures are built or installed by cabinetmakers.

Cabinetmakers who work on remodeling projects might wish to pursue certifications from the National Association of the Remodeling Industry (NARI).

FLOOR COVERER

Floor coverers are carpenters that work exclusively with flooring materials. They start their work after other workers install plywood subfloors over the floor frame. Floor coverers must be good at taking accurate measurements and estimating supplies and costs. They work with a variety of materials, including carpet, ceramic tiles, vinyl, and wood. They also have an extensive knowledge of the adhesives, fasteners, and wood stains needed to finish flooring a room. Many floorers are adept at restoring old, worn-out flooring.

A floor coverer needs to be familiar with the range of products available so they can install a floor that looks good, is safe, and will be durable for its use and location.

As part of their apprenticeship, floor coverers might become certified by the International Standards & Training Alliance (INSTALL). Those who specialize in wood flooring can seek certification from the National Wood Flooring Association (NWFA). These certifications reassure customers that the carpenter is fully trained in the latest techniques and materials.

Professional floor coverers know there's more to a good floor than meets the eye. The layers you don't see ensure that the floor will be safe and beautiful.

INTERIOR SYSTEMS SPECIALIST

Interior systems specialists are most often employed by commercial building contractors. They assemble and install metal frames for ceiling tiles and lights. They also install acoustical tiles, office furnishings, wall partitions, and other items used in commercial buildings. They must be familiar with fire codes and noise standards. They often work on health-care facilities which are designed to contain pathogens and contaminants from being transmitted through the building.

Although most of the time they install prefabricated materials, interior systems specialists should have fabrication and welding skills to help solve unforeseen problems. Although they work indoors, they may work on scaffolds to install ceiling systems.

MILLWRIGHT

Millwrights install, maintain, and repair machinery. The machines they work with can include conveyor systems, electric sensors, generators, pumps, and turbines. Some millwrights specialize in one specific type of machine. Millwrights need to have a solid understanding of industrial tools and mechanics.

Millwrights set up the necessary machinery for a carpentry job before it begins. While the job is in progress, they maintain the machinery to ensure that work is not interrupted. They oil moving parts, repair machinery when necessary, maintain electrical connections, and refill fuel tanks. They may also be called upon to fabricate new parts on

The word *millwright* dates to the 14th century. Wooden mills like this one were powered by water. The moving water turned a large wheel on the outside of the mill, which turned the wooden gears inside the mill to perform whatever task the mill was built for.

the job site. In addition to the machines themselves, millwrights oversee construction of the foundations needed to support the machinery. When a job is done, millwrights oversee the workers who take apart and move machinery.

They also install heavy machinery in places such as factories and power plants. They may be required to instruct workers in the daily use and care of all machinery on the site.

It's common for a millwright to perform another kind of specialized work, such as serving as a cabinetmaker.

PILE DRIVER

A pile driver operates large construction vehicles that pound wood or steel beams into the ground. These beams, called piles, are mainly used to create support systems for large buildings and structures. Along with basic carpentry skills, particularly concrete formwork, pile drivers need to be knowledgeable about topics such as bedrock formations, construction vehicles, foundation materials, metals, and welding.

Besides creating support structures for large buildings, pile drivers also create the foundations for piers and bridges. Pile drivers might be needed to help hold back land during deep excavations. Similarly, they are sometimes used to drive piles that hold back water when creating underwater bridge and pier foundations. This can require additional specialized certifications such as commercial diving and underwater welding. Their job is critical to the safety of everyone working on the site. Pile drivers often work alone, but are in frequent contact with engineers, supervisors, and surveyors.

These concrete piles will eventually hold up a bridge. The person who installs them is also considered a carpenter.

Scenic carpenters bring a designer's vision to life and transport audiences to faraway places. Theatrical sets may involve special effects, moving sections of the stage, and sections of walls that move throughout the course of the show.

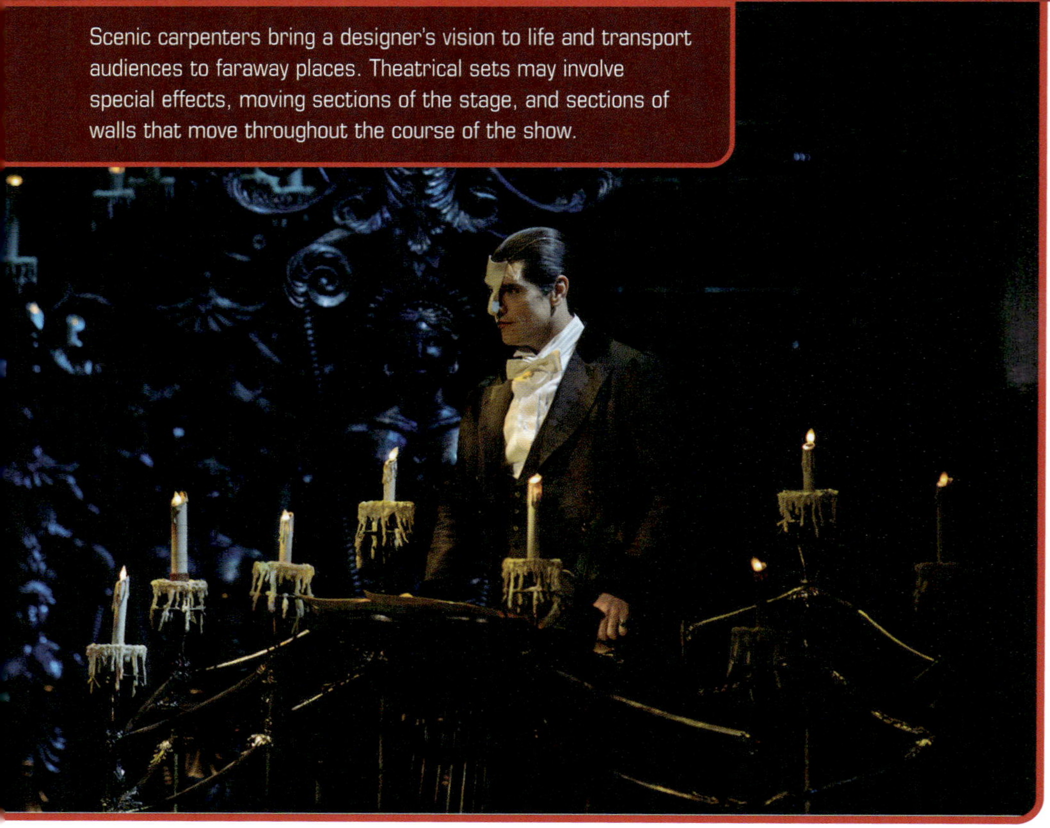

PROP AND STAGE DESIGN

Carpenters interested in working in the entertainment industry might want to help build props and stages. These carpenters are sometimes known as set carpenters or scenic carpenters. Stage designers and builders help create sets for amusement parks, movie productions, and theatrical shows. A general carpentry apprenticeship can help people who want to pursue a career in prop and stage design establish themselves. However, there are also prop and stage design apprenticeships.

Theater sets transport the audience to far off times and places—or maybe just to Granny's kitchen.

It all depends on the show that's being produced and the designer's vision. Besides looking good, a set must be safe and functional. There may be doors and windows that open and shut, and stairs that actors walk on. There may be platforms that actors will walk or dance on. The set must be sturdy enough for all the actions the audience sees, and maybe even some that it doesn't. Stagehands might need to access things from behind the set. There needs to be enough clearance for people to access fire exits and allow for emergency personnel and equipment.

Some set carpenters will work in a single location, such as a theater or a park. Others, however, will have the opportunity to travel to different locations. This is especially true for carpenters that work on touring theatrical productions or movies. Some movies are filmed entirely on a set, but many are filmed in various locations. Set carpenters often take great pleasure in seeing their creations become an important part of a movie or theatrical production.

IATSE represents carpenters who work in the entertainment industry.

Theatre sets also need to be safe, sturdy, and meet local fire and electrical codes. The set may need to stand for years in a Broadway production, or be disassembled, or struck, after only a few performances in a small venue. Sets for a touring show need to be taken apart quickly, loaded onto a truck, then reassembled at the next theatre.

WHAT'S NEXT?

Trained carpenters can gain promotions or move on to a completely new career. Career changes often come with greater responsibility and more work, but they can also come with more benefits, authority, and a higher salary.

For example, carpenters who have several years of experience working in multiple areas of construction may move up to a supervisory or management position, such as a foreman or superintendent. A foreman supervises all workers in his or her trade, so there are always multiple foremen on any large job site. Superintendents direct all daily activities onsite, and foremen may report directly to them. Often these positions are available to college graduates with specific training in construction management.

Becoming a foreman might require taking additional classes, as well as the OSHA 30 certification.

The UBC sponsors a superintendent career training program called the Carpenters International Training Fund's Superintendent Career Training Program (SCTP). This program is similar to the UBC's apprenticeship program. The program selects carpenters based on their experience and standing in the union. They must have completed OSHA's 30-hour safety program or the Canadian equivalent. Participants receive classroom training for 18 months. After that, they are assigned a mentor who tests them in the field.

GOING INTO BUSINESS FOR YOURSELF

Many trained carpenters decide to start their own businesses. Some carpenters with extensive commercial and residential building experience choose to become contractors.

A contractor is a person or company that signs a contract to complete a project. Contractors bid on potential carpentry jobs. The contractor that puts in the lowest bid generally gets the job. Contracting is a competitive business, and it can be difficult for small companies and first-time contractors to break into the business. Some seasons may be slower than others, so contractors must be prepared to endure occasional financial losses. Still, contractors can make a lot of money if they work hard and build a good reputation for themselves.

A general contractor is one who handles all aspects of a building job. If special workers, such as plumbers or painters are needed, the contractor

BUILDING A HOUSE

From start to finish, building a new house takes about three to six months. Of course, this is subject to things such as weather, availability of supplies, and permits being in good order.

The first step is to prepare the building site by making sure the area for the foundation is level. Once the foundation is laid, it may need to be checked by a building inspector before construction continues.

Next, framers will begin to assemble the skeleton of the house. They'll be followed by plumbers, electricians, and heating, ventilation, and air conditioning (HVAC) technicians. Workers add insulation and drywall after all the pipes and ducts are in place. Cabinetmakers and finishers will install stairs, closets, and interior doors. Windows, doors, and the roof will be constructed. Next, sinks, toilets and floor coverings will be installed.

Once construction is complete, a building inspector will go over the house and issue a certificate of occupancy. After that, you'll do a walk-through with your contractor.

Having a house built to your specification involves a lot of steps, but it can be easier than renovating an existing structure. Perhaps you need a home that's wheelchair accessible. Or maybe you want a ground floor suite for an elderly parent. Building a new, energy-efficient home might make more sense than ripping out old insulation or wiring and replacing lots of windows.

A building inspector is usually a local government employee. Their job is to make sure that structures follow the building codes. These codes ensure that buildings are safe. For instance, a building code might specify how many exits are required in a house, or that doors in a public building are wide enough for wheelchairs.

hires them as subcontractors. Materials, labor, and any subcontractors' bills are combined into one invoice. The client only has to deal with and pay the general contractor.

Other contractors might opt for a very niche business, such as replacing bathtubs. Often these companies are very good at what they do, but if you need any other work done in your bathroom, you need to seek out a separate contractor.

Some carpenters might choose to move away from the construction industry all together. They might choose to run small specialty business, such as a woodshop that specializes in creating and repairing furniture.

There is a lot for carpenters to think about when starting their own business. Businesspeople must understand local laws and regulations. For example, some states require special licenses to do large-scale carpentry and construction; others don't. Business owners in every state must have insurance.

It's in a contractor's best interest to understand all facets of building construction—including carpentry, electrical wiring, plumbing, and so on. Contractors also must deal with things such as billing, hiring employees, and ordering supplies. Some contractors hire foremen and supervisors to help oversee large projects. Starting a business is a lot of work, but for a person who wants to be his or her own boss, it can be worth it.

WHAT ELSE CAN I DO?

Instead of becoming a contractor, many carpenters choose to become private businesspeople. They place advertisements in online directories or through social media. Most of their time is spent traveling with their tools to homes and buildings to build and repair a wide variety of projects.

Some carpenters choose to become instructors or teachers. Others use their knowledge as purchasing agents working for contractors or even architects. Some specialized carpenters may assemble teams of workers in their area and start their own business. For example, a cabinetmaker may open his or her own shop and bid on construction projects. After getting a job, the team of cabinetmakers that works for the shop would go to job sites and do their job.

A carpenter might even explore a new specialty, such as marine carpentry, if they live near water. In short, the career choices for a carpenter are almost limitless.

THE LOCAL HANDYPERSON

In today's economic climate, not everyone can be guaranteed a steady and secure job. Fortunately, there are usually many different types of jobs that a trained carpenter can apply for, even during tough economic times. Even with a secure full-time job, however, a carpenter can use his or her skills to earn supplemental income by doing smaller jobs on the side. This can especially come in handy when a carpenter needs to catch up on his or her bills, buy new tools and supplies, save up for a vacation, or just wants to make some extra money to buy something special. Depending on a carpenter's experience level, supplementing his or her income can be accomplished in any number of ways—from

LIVING HISTORY MUSEUMS

An interesting career option for a carpenter who loves history and working with their hands might be a job at a living history museum or historic house. This type of museum can consist of a single house, a homestead with outbuildings, or an entire village.

At large living history museums such as Colonial Williamsburg, museum educators learn historic trades and wood crafts and demonstrate them to the public.

If you prefer to work behind the scenes, any collection of vintage buildings requires special care and maintenance. Museums conduct extensive research so that any necessary repairs blend in with the character of the building and site. This might entail sourcing particular types of wood or hardware.

Practitioners of Historic Trades at Colonial Williamsburg serve an apprenticeship under one of the town's master craftsmen. They learn their trade in front of the general public, wearing historic reproduction clothing and using 18th century techniques and reproduction tools.

fixing a neighbor's creaky staircase to building a toolshed for a client.

Most often, carpenters get extra work through word of mouth. Carpenters often hear things like, "I heard you're a carpenter. I've been looking for someone to fix the roof of my garage. How much would you charge for something like that?" Those are exciting words for a carpenter who wants to pick up some extra work. Carpenters can also drum up business by advertising their services online or via social media. Another option is to register on a site such as TaskRabbit.com or Handy.com. People use these sites when they need to hire someone for a small project, such as assembling furniture or completing a small repair.

Every client that a carpenter does a good job for becomes a valuable connection in his or her network, especially if they leave a good review online. Any job, no matter how small, might somehow lead to bigger jobs later on. Picking up side work is also a great way to practice the craft of carpentry. Some carpenters choose to start their own business based on the experience they gain doing side jobs.

A BRIGHT HORIZON

The future looks good for carpenters. Despite occasional setbacks in the economy, carpenters are always in high demand. As the demand for new buildings continues, carpenters will be needed at nearly every step of the construction process. The BLS projects over 90,000 job openings for carpenters per year for the next decade.

Home remodeling is another lucrative area for carpenters today. Old homes often have problems that can only be repaired by a trained carpenter. Sometimes walls were built around the original furnace. Replacing it means taking down walls and then replacing them. Wiring or insulation may need updating, possibly requiring walls to be opened and then repaired.

Some carpenters make a good living buying old homes, fixing them up, and selling them for a great profit. The home industry alone sustains literally millions of carpenters.

As technology changes, so does carpentry. New tools, supplies, and techniques have revolutionized the way carpenters do their job. Those who have been in the business for a long time might be required to change and update their craft. New carpenters receive modern training, preparing them for a career in the field.

Environmentally conscious home buyers want to reduce their carbon footprint. They're interested in clean energy sources, such as solar panels.

Today, people are very conscious of climate change and the impact of their activities on planet Earth. Construction industry professionals need to be up on all the latest innovations, such as solar panels and low-emissivity windows, which reduce heat transfer.

Conscientious consumers also look for buildings constructed with recycled or reclaimed materials, fast-growth woods such as bamboo, or timber from sustainable forests. They also expect energy-efficient appliances and water-efficient plumbing fixtures.

Home buyers also expect their new house to be prepared for the installation of all sorts of technology. Computers and high-speed internet are a part of daily life. Smart appliances that can be controlled from a phone or tablet are becoming more common, as are smart security systems.

Despite changes to the profession, in many ways carpentry has stayed largely the same for centuries. Carpenters listen to what people want, then they build it. Whether you want to build an affordable home for a family, the next high-tech skyscraper, or restore vintage furniture, there's a career for you.

Hemp is a safe, environmentally smart insulation material. It's organic, renewable, and compostable.

10 GREAT QUESTIONS TO ASK A CONSTRUCTION PROFESSIONAL

Here are some questions you can ask a construction professional. If more than one specialty interests you, see if you can find a professional in that field to speak to.

1. Is it true I can get paid while I train to be a carpenter?
2. Did you go to college or train as an apprentice?
3. Are there any high school classes or activities you recommend?
4. Why did you choose your specialty? Do you have more than one?
5. Are you an independent contractor or do you work for a company?
6. Are there any books you recommend I read? Are there any industry blogs or magazines that are worth following?
7. Has your job changed because of climate change?
8. Did you go back to school to learn about new technology or green building techniques?
9. Do you have any certifications from agencies besides the UBC? Which ones would you recommend I get?
10. Is there anything you wish someone had told you when you were considering this career?

What other questions can you think of?

Whether you want to craft wooden furniture using old-world techniques, or build the latest high-tech skyscrapers, there are plenty of great career paths available to you as a trained carpenter.

GLOSSARY

associate's degree: A two-year degree from a college.

blueprint: A photographic print of a technical drawing.

certify: To officially say that someone has met certain standards or requirements.

commercial: Relating to the world of business.

contractor: A company or individual with a formal contract to do a specific job. Contractors supply labor, materials, and management staff during a job.

drywall: A type of wall board made of sheets of plaster pressed together.

fabricate: To make or construct.

fiberglass: A lightweight, durable building material made from compressed glass fibers.

Formica: A strong plastic sheet used to protect surfaces.

hemp: A plant used to make rope, insulation, and fabric.

industry: A group of businesses that provide a certain product or service.

joiner: A carpenter trained to make cuts in wood so that they fit together snugly without the use of nails or screws. Also used to describe carpenters who manufacture objects that need to have wood joints, such as door and window frames.

plumb bob: A pointed weight suspended on the end of a string. Plumb bobs are used to create perfectly straight vertical reference lines.

prefabricated: Something that is manufactured in separate components that are intended to be assembled later.

residential: Relating to private housing.

restoration: To return something to the way it looked when it was first made.

scaffold: A temporary framework of poles and planks used to support workers and their supplies.

strike: When employees stop working as a group in order to protest a company's practices.

suspended ceiling: A secondary ceiling hung below the main structural ceiling, which usually hides piping, wiring, and ductwork. Also called a dropped or false ceiling.

sustainable: Able to last a long time.

timber frame: A kind of building constructed by fitting wooden beams together without nails and screws.

vocation: A job or profession.

FOR MORE INFORMATION

ASSOCIATED BUILDERS AND CONTRACTORS (ABC)

440 1st St., N.W., Suite 200
Washington, D.C. 20001
(202) 595-1505
Website: www.abc.org
Facebook and Twitter: @ABCNational
Instagram: @abc_national
The ABC is a trade association that represents the construction industry to government agencies and news media.

ASSOCIATED GENERAL CONTRACTORS OF AMERICA (AGC)

2300 Wilson Blvd., Suite 300
Arlington, VA 22201
(703) 548-3118
Website: www.agc.org
Facebook and Twitter: @AGCofA
The AGC is an organization dedicated to improving the safety and quality of construction work in the United States.

CANADIAN CONSTRUCTION ASSOCIATION (CCA)

250 Albert Street, Suite 300
Ottawa, ON K1P 6M1
Canada
(613) 236-9455
Website: www.cca-acc.com
Twitter: @ConstructionCAN
The CCA is the voice of the businesses, contractors, and suppliers involved in the Canadian commercial and industrial construction industry.

CANADIAN HOME BUILDERS' ASSOCIATION (CHBA)

141 Laurier Ave. West, Suite 500
Ottawa, ON K1P 5J3
Canada
(613) 230-3060
Website: www.chba.ca
Facebook, Instagram, and Twitter: *@chbanational*
The CHBA represents the segment of Canada's construction industry concerned with residential building.

EMPLOYMENT AND TRAINING ADMINISTRATION (ETA) U.S. DEPARTMENT OF LABOR

Frances Perkins Building
200 Constitution Avenue N.W.
Washington, D.C. 20210
(877) US-2JOBS [872-5627]
Website: www.doleta.gov

The ETA is part of the Department of Labor. It oversees job training and employment-assistance programs, which are generally administered at a local government level.

HOME BUILDERS INSTITUTE (HBI)

1201 15th Street NW, Sixth Floor
Washington, D.C. 20005
(202) 371-0600
Website: www.hbi.org
Facebook and Instagram: @HBIBuildingcareers
Twitter: @HBIBuildCareers
The HBI provides free pre-apprenticeship training in the trades.

JOB CORPS

200 Constitution Avenue NW, Room N4459
Washington, D.C. 20210
(800) 733-JOBS [5627]
Website: www.jobcorps.gov
Facebook, Instagram, and Twitter: @DOLJobCorps
The Job Corps is Department of Labor program that provides free job training for young people.

NATIONAL ASSOCIATION OF WOMEN IN CONSTRUCTION (NAWIC)

327 S. Adams Street
Fort Worth, TX 76104
(800) 552-3506

Website: www.nawic.org
Facebook, Instagram, and Twitter: @nawicnational
The NAWIC was offers education and networking opportunities to women in the construction industry.

UNITED BROTHERHOOD OF CARPENTERS AND JOINERS OF AMERICA (UBC)

International Headquarters
101 Constitution Ave NW
Washington, D.C. 20001
Website: carpenters.org
Facebook: @CarpentersUnited
Instagram: @UBCJA
Twitter: @UBCJA_Official
The UBC is one of North America's largest construction trade unions, with membership across the US and Canada.

FOR FURTHER READING

Astbury, Jon. *The Architecture Book*. New York, NY: DK, 2023.

Collins, Corbin. *Skilled Trade Professionals: A Practical Career Guide*. Lanham, MD: Rowman & Littlefield, 2019.

DK Publishing Inc. *Woodworking: The Complete Step-by-Step Manual*. New York, NY: DK Publishing, 2020.

Hughes, Karl, and Jennifer Wisdom. *Millennials' Guide to the Construction Trades: What No One Ever Told You About a Career in Construction*. Winding Pathway Books, 2020.

Lussier, Georgian, and William Lussier. *Building Success in the Trades: Career Advice for Students, Parents, Educators and Experienced Tradespeople*. Independently Published, 2019.

Skourtis, Pantelis. *Design a House with AutoCAD Architecture*. Independently Published, 2021.

Willkens, Danielle. *Architecture for Teens: A Beginner's Book for Aspiring Architects*. Emeryville, CA: Rockridge Press, 2021.

INDEX

E

F

G

H

I

J

L

M

ABOUT THE AUTHOR

KATHLEEN A. KLATTE is the author of many nonfiction books for children and teens. Topics range from animals and nature to constitutional law to unusual career choices. She lives in New York with one cat and far too many books and Legos.

PHOTO CREDITS

Photo credits: Cover, p. 1 Robert Kneschke/Shutterstock.com; p.3-96 Merydolla// Shutterstock.com; p. 4 Viktor Osipenko/Shutterstock.com; p. 5 Gorodenkoff/ Shutterstock.com; p. 7 https://commons.wikimedia.org/wiki/File:Norm_Abram_and_The_New_Yankee_Workshop_tries_out_a_tool_used_in_space_while_wearing_gloves_that_are_part_of_the_spacewalking_suits.jpg; p. 8 RPBaiao/ Shutterstock.com; p. 9 RPBaiao/Shutterstock.com; p. 13 OlegD/Shutterstock.com; p.15 gpointstudio/Shutterstock.com; p. 17 Platoo Studio/Shutterstock.com; p. 18 Nomad_Soul/Shutterstock.com; pp. 19, 53 Rawpixel.com/Shutterstock.com; p. 21 ZikG/Shutterstock.com; p.22 Jesus Cervantes/Shutterstock.com; pp. 24. 37 Monkey Business Images/Shutterstock.com; p. 30 Gorodenkoff/Shutterstock.com; p. 31 Glynnis Jones/Shutterstock.com; p. 33 Stephanie L Sanchez/Shutterstock.com; p. 35 Rob Crandall/Shutterstock.com; p. 39 JHVEPhoto/Shutterstock.com; p. 41 Simo Sepp/Shutterstock.com; p. 42 RossHelen/Shutterstock.com; p. 46 Ververidis Vasilis/Shutterstock.com; p. 47 Stock-Asso/Shutterstock.com; p. 48 Bruno de Gois/Shutterstock.com; p. 51 https://commons.wikimedia.org/wiki/File:New_York_State_Department_of_Labor.svg; p. 55 FabrikaSimf/Shutterstock.com; p. 57 Andrey_Popov/Shutterstock.com; p. 58 NassornSnitwong/Shutterstock.com; p. 59 Gustavo Frazao/Shutterstock.com; p. 60 MIND AND I/Shutterstock.com; p.61 Trong Nguyen/Shutterstock.com; p. 62 AXL/Shutterstock.com; p. 63 Francescomoufotografo/Shutterstock.com; p. 64 ungvar/Shutterstock.com; p. 66 Hananeko_Studio/Shutterstock.com; p. 68 dita dumitru/Shutterstock.com; p.69 Tricky_Shark/Shutterstock.com;p. 70 BW Press/Shutterstock.com; p. 71 aerogondo2/Shutterstock.com;p. 72 MilanMarkovic78/Shutterstock.com; p. 75 Sean Locke Photography/Shutterstock.com; p. 78 Daniel Reiner/Shutterstock.com; p. 80 kckate16/Shutterstock.com; p. 81 Olga_Ionina/Shutterstock.com; p. 83 NTshutterth/Shutterstock.com.